# Laura Ingalls Wilder

by Ginger Wadsworth
illustrations by Shelly O. Haas

Carolrhoda Books, Inc./Minneapolis

*for Jean, dear friend*          *— G.W.*

*for my mother, who blesses our family with*
*the art of storytelling, and Grandfather,*
*who inspired her mastery*          *— S.O.H.*

Text copyright © 2000 by Ginger Wadsworth
Illustrations copyright © 2000 by Shelly O. Haas

*This book is available in two editions:*
Library edition by Carolrhoda Books, Inc.
Soft cover by First Avenue Editions
Divisions of the Lerner Publishing Group
241 First Avenue North
Minneapolis, MN 55401 U.S.A.

Website address: www.lernerbooks.com


Library of Congress Cataloging-in-Publication Data

Wadsworth, Ginger.
    Laura Ingalls Wilder / by Ginger Wadsworth ; illustrations by
  Shelly O. Haas.
      p. cm. — (Carolrhoda on my own books)
    Summary: Examines Laura Ingalls Wilder's life as a pioneer girl and
  her work as a writer describing that life for others.
    ISBN 1-57505-266-0 (lib. bdg.)
    ISBN 1-57505-423-X (pbk.)
    1. Wilder, Laura Ingalls, 1867–1957—Juvenile literature. 2. Women
  authors, American—20th century—Biography—Juvenile literature.
  3. Children's stories—Authorship—Juvenile literature. 4. Frontier
  and pioneer life—Juvenile literature. [1. Wilder, Laura Ingalls,
  1867–1957. 2. Authors, American. 3. Women—Biography. 4. Frontier
  and pioneer life.] I. Haas, Shelly O., ill. II. Title.
  III. Series.
  PS3545.I342Z92   2000
  813'.52—dc21                                    99-21333
  [B]

Manufactured in the United States of America
1 2 3 4 5 6 – SP – 05 04 03 02 01 00

*Minnesota*
*1874*

Seven-year-old Laura scrambled
into the covered wagon.
Her big sister, Mary, climbed in beside her.
Her little sister, Carrie, sat on Ma's lap.
Pa shook the reins, and the horses pulled
the wagon down the dusty road.

Day after day,

the covered wagon rolled west.

Ma's cookpot banged

against the wagon bed.

The white canvas top snapped in the wind.

Mary, Laura, and Carrie played

with their corncob dolls in the wagon bed.

Jack, the bulldog, ran behind the wagon.

Laura liked to look outside.

The sky seemed to fit over the prairie

like a big blue bowl.

At night, the Ingalls family often camped
beside a creek.

Ma cooked beans and meat over a campfire.

After supper, Laura wiped the tin plates
and cups and put them away.

Pa kept his rifle nearby.

He would need his rifle
if a wolf came too close to the campfire.

As they sat around the fire,
Pa played his fiddle.

And they all sang along.

Laura begged Pa to tell a story.

Pa scratched his shaggy beard.

Laura thought he might tell the story
about the big bear in the woods.

Instead, Pa began to tell about Grandpa
and the panther.

It was one of Laura's favorites
because it was so scary.

Each time Pa told it,
she shivered.

Laura liked Pa's stories.

She had heard them over and over again.

Maybe tonight she could tell the ending.

In the end, as always,

Grandpa got away from the panther.

Just like Pa, Laura was a good storyteller.

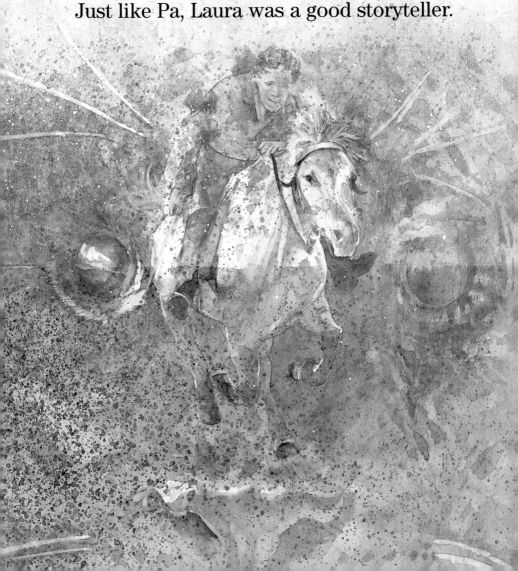

*Dakota Territory*
*1880*

Laura peeked out the door of the shanty.

The prairie grasses seemed to dance

with the wind.

Laura hurried through her chores.

She straightened the quilt

on the trundle bed she shared with Mary.

Then she made breakfast for Carrie

and baby Grace.

She mended a rip in a sheet,

but she did not like to sew.

Finally the inside work was done!
Laura raced out of the tiny house.
She ran barefoot over the dark prairie dirt.
She pushed off her sunbonnet.
The warm sun felt good on her face.
Laura hoped Ma would not scold her
for being unladylike.

She moved Ellen, the cow, to fresh grass.

Then she helped Pa cut hay.

They raked the hay into rows to dry.

They bundled the dry hay.

Then they carried the bundles into the barn.

The hay would feed the cows
during the long, cold winter.
Even though she was short,
Laura was strong.
She liked to help Pa
with some of the hard farmwork.

At last, Laura filled the brown jug
with water and carried it inside the house.
Mary sang as she dusted.
For Laura, it was easy to forget
that Mary had become blind.

Laura and Mary put on their sunbonnets.

Arm in arm, they followed

an old buffalo trail across the prairie.

Mary was brave about being blind.

So Laura tried to be brave, too.

She had promised Pa

that she would become Mary's eyes.

Laura would tell Mary
about everything she saw.
While they walked, Laura told Mary
about the pink flowers covering the prairie
like a carpet.
Wild cloud horses ran across the blue sky.
Laura painted other pictures with words
for her sister.

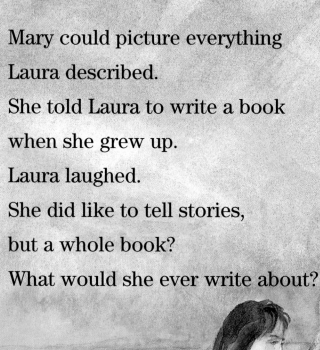

Mary could picture everything
Laura described.
She told Laura to write a book
when she grew up.
Laura laughed.
She did like to tell stories,
but a whole book?
What would she ever write about?

Someday, Mary said, houses and towns
would cover the prairie.
Roads would crisscross the prairie
instead of buffalo trails.
Mary told Laura to write down
Pa's pioneer stories.
Laura laughed again.
Who would want to read
about the Ingalls family?

*From South Dakota to Missouri*
*1880s and 1890s*

When Laura was 18 years old, she married

Almanzo Wilder.

He owned a big wheat farm.

It was hard work being a farmer's wife,

but Laura was happy.

Laura and Almanzo had a daughter.

They named her Rose

for the wild prairie roses.

Laura helped Almanzo plant wheat.

Soon, green shoots poked out
of the dark soil.

Before long,
their feathered tops blew in the wind.

The wheat needed rain to grow.

That year, a hail storm crushed the wheat.

The next summer,
the prairie was hot and dry.
The heat was like the inside of Laura's oven
on baking days.
Without rain, the wheat turned brown.
It dried in the fields.

The summer after that,

millions of grasshoppers ate the wheat.

They ate all the vegetables in the garden.

Then Laura and Almanzo's house

burned down.

Laura tried to be brave.

Laura and Almanzo decided to move
to Missouri.
They wanted to start over.
They packed their wagon
with pots and pans, beds, and clothes.
Seven-year-old Rose climbed in.
Laura hugged Ma and Pa and her sisters
good-bye.
Everyone cried and promised to write.

Two horses pulled the covered wagon
down the dusty road.
Laura and Almanzo sang songs
to make the long days go by more quickly.
Rose asked Laura to tell her stories.
So Laura did.
She told Rose about when baby Grace
had disappeared in the tall prairie grass.
She told about celebrating Christmas
with her cousins in the Big Woods
of Wisconsin.

After supper, Laura sat by the campfire
with her notebook and pencil.
She was keeping a diary of their trip.
She described the farms they saw.

She wrote about the long lines
of covered wagons going back and forth
across the prairie.
Other pioneers were also trying
to find good farms.

After 45 days on the road,

the Wilders reached Mansfield, Missouri.

At first, they camped in the woods

near town.

Then they found a small farm to buy.

The farm had rolling hills

covered with trees.

Big rocks were everywhere.

Laura named their farm Rocky Ridge.

They moved into the one-room cabin.

Laura swept out spiders' webs, leaves,

and mouse nests.

For safekeeping, she put her notebook

into a trunk.

Someday she would write

about her new life.

Laura and Almanzo made a good team.
They cut down some trees
with a big crosscut saw.
Almanzo sold a wagonload of wood in town
for 75 cents.

Laura sold some eggs and a bucket
of wild berries for 10 cents.
It had been a long time
since they had had so much money.
Laura whistled happily as she worked.

*San Francisco*
*1915*

When Laura was 48, she took a train
from Missouri to San Francisco, California.
She was eager to see
her grown-up daughter, Rose.
Rose had become a writer.

Laura was still a farmer's wife,
but she also wrote stories for newspapers.
The train to California seemed to go so fast.
Laura remembered going West
in a covered wagon years before.
The wagon had taken weeks
to cross the prairie.
It only took a few days for the train
to get all the way to California.

Laura and Rose waded
in the Pacific Ocean.
They walked through a grove
of redwood trees.
They took a streetcar
up and down the steep hills.
San Francisco was a beautiful city.
Even so, Laura missed Almanzo.
She wrote to him almost every day.

Laura tried to describe everything
just as she saw it.
She wrote about driving around
in Rose's little red car.
She wrote about watching the sun set
over the ocean.
Almanzo saved every letter from Laura.
He tied them up with string and put them
in a box.

*Rocky Ridge Farm*
*1930s*

Before she knew it, Laura turned 60.

She had gray hair, but she did not feel old.

Busy as she was, Laura wanted to write

about her days as a pioneer girl.

Laura put some bread in the oven to bake.

She sat down at her desk.

Where should she begin?

In the Big Woods?

On Plum Creek?

In Dakota Territory?

Laura thought of Pa and his jolly laugh.

She missed gentle, quiet Ma.

Like Pa, Laura had a good memory.

She was a good storyteller.

But she had never written down

any of her childhood stories.

Laura picked up her pencil

and began to write about the Big Woods.

Laura pictured the two giant oak trees
that shaded the house in the woods.
Under the oak trees, she and Mary
had put on tea parties with their dolls.
All around the house and beyond
were more and more trees.
Laura could almost hear Pa's ax
in the woods.
Laura wrote about other little houses.
One house had been beside a creek.
Another was at the edge of a lake.
Laura still fixed meals, made butter,
and helped Almanzo with the farmwork.
When she had time, she wrote.
Sometimes she remembered a story
in the middle of the night.
She would jump out of bed
and hurry to her desk to write it down.

When Laura finally finished,

she mailed the stories to Rose.

Rose sent the stories to a publishing house.

They liked the stories.

But they wanted some changes.

Laura sat down at her desk again.

This time, she just wrote

about her memories in her first house.

"Once upon a time,

sixty years ago, a little girl lived

in the Big Woods of Wisconsin,

in a little gray house made of logs."

*Little House in the Big Woods*
was published when Laura was 65.
She did not dream of becoming famous.
But she hoped that a few children
would read about her adventures
in the Big Woods.

Lots and lots of children loved *Little House in the Big Woods.*

Readers all over the United States wrote to Laura.

They asked her what happened next.

They wanted to know all about Ma, Pa, Mary, Laura, Carrie, and Grace.

They wanted to know about Almanzo, too.

Once more, Laura sat down at her desk.

She had a good idea for the next book,

and the next, and the next.

Each book would be

about a different little house.

After all, she had moved many times.

Laura picked up her pencil again.

46

## Afterword

Laura wrote seven more "Little House" books. She and Almanzo continued to enjoy their farm and the beautiful Ozark Mountains. Every day, Laura and her bulldog, Old Ben, walked a half-mile to the mailbox. Laura carried home a big basket of fan letters. Most of the letters came from children who had read her books. Laura answered every letter.

Laura died in 1957 when she was 90 years old, but she will never be forgotten. Many of her Little Houses are preserved as museums. Millions of children still read Laura's books about her pioneer days as a little girl. They are special books about a special pioneer.

# Important Dates

January 10, 1865—Mary Ingalls is born in Wisconsin.

February 7, 1867—Laura Ingalls is born in Wisconsin.

August 3, 1870—Carrie Ingalls is born in Kansas.

May 23, 1877—Grace Ingalls is born in Iowa.

1879—The Ingalls family settles in Dakota Territory.

August 25, 1885—Laura marries Almanzo Wilder.

December 5, 1886—Rose Wilder is born.

1894—The Wilder family moves to Missouri.

1909—Rose moves to San Francisco.

1911—Laura publishes first newspaper article,
     in *Missouri Ruralist.*

1915—Laura visits Rose in San Francisco.

1932—*Little House in the Big Woods* is published.

1933—*Farmer Boy* is published.

1935—*Little House on the Prairie* is published.

1937—*On the Banks of Plum Creek* is published.

1939—*By the Shores of Silver Lake* is published.

1940—*The Long Winter* is published.

1941—*Little Town on the Prairie* is published.

1943—*These Happy Golden Years* is published.

October 23, 1949—Almanzo dies at the age of 92.

February 10, 1957—Laura dies at the age of 90.